NATIONAL GEOGRAPHIC

M000005986

Which One Does Not Belong?

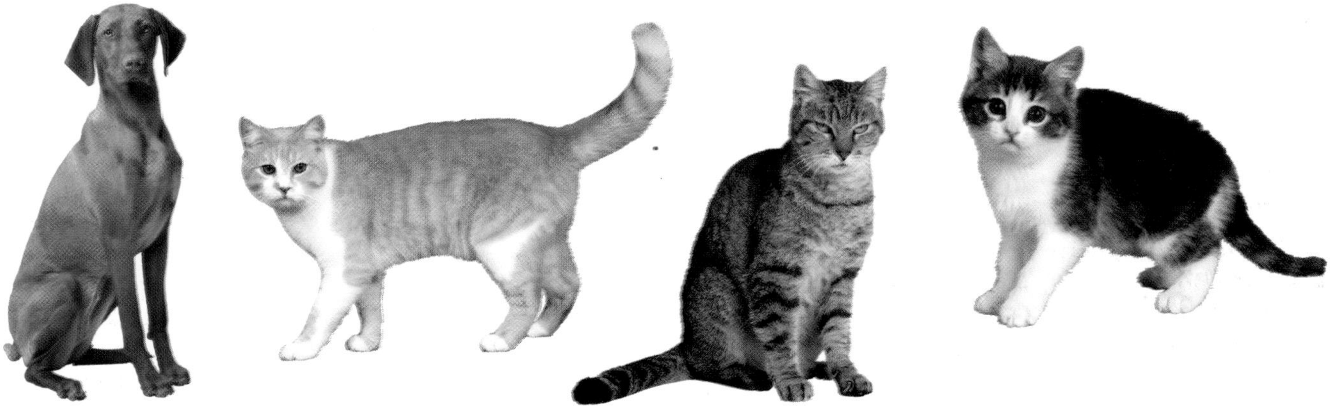

Kevin Biggs

Which one does not belong?

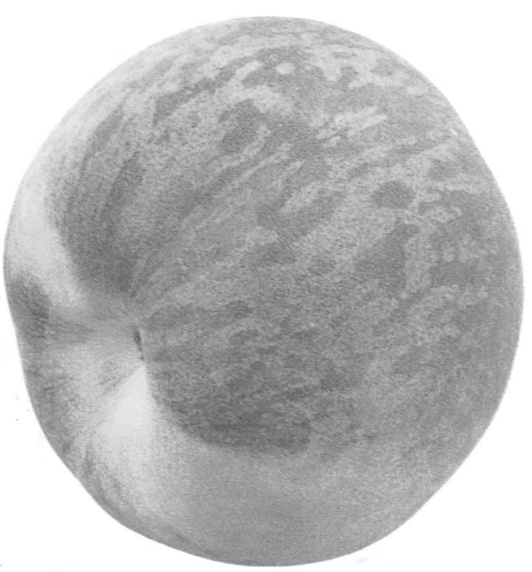

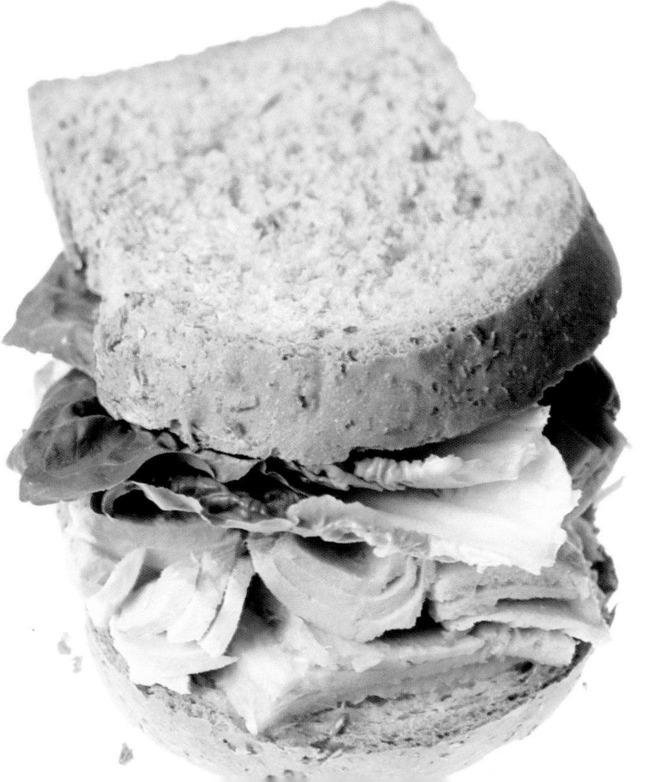

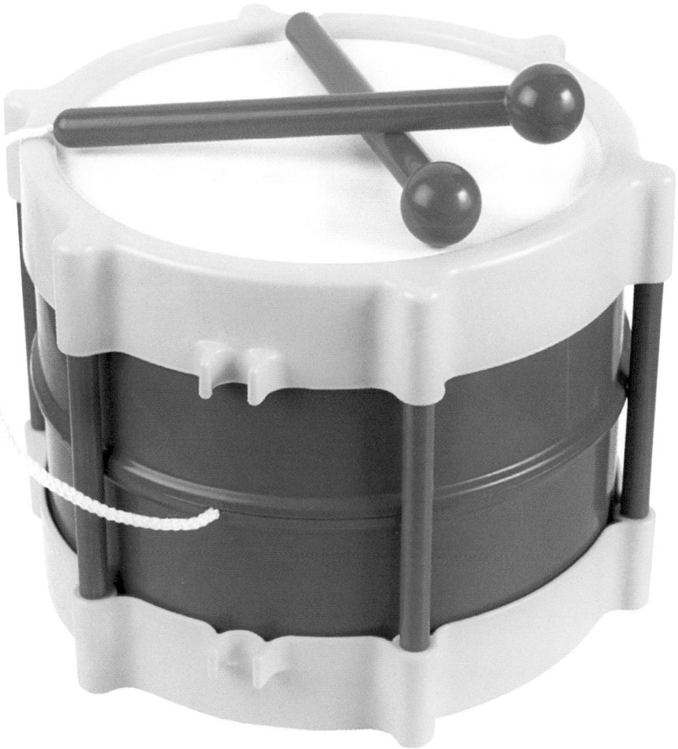

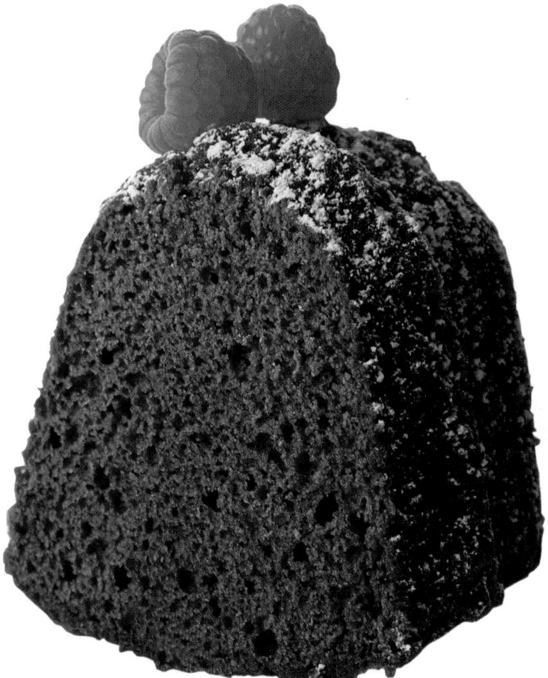

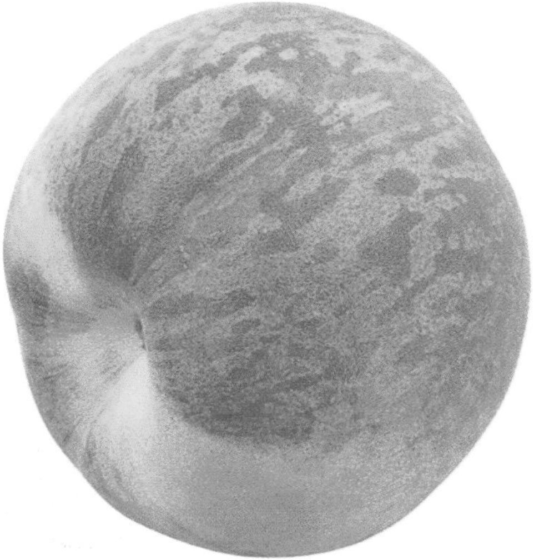

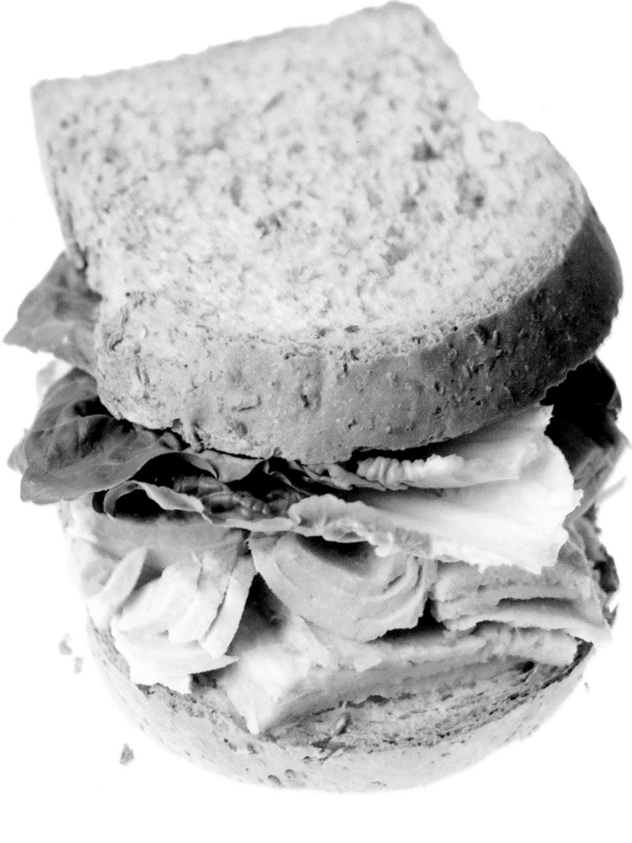

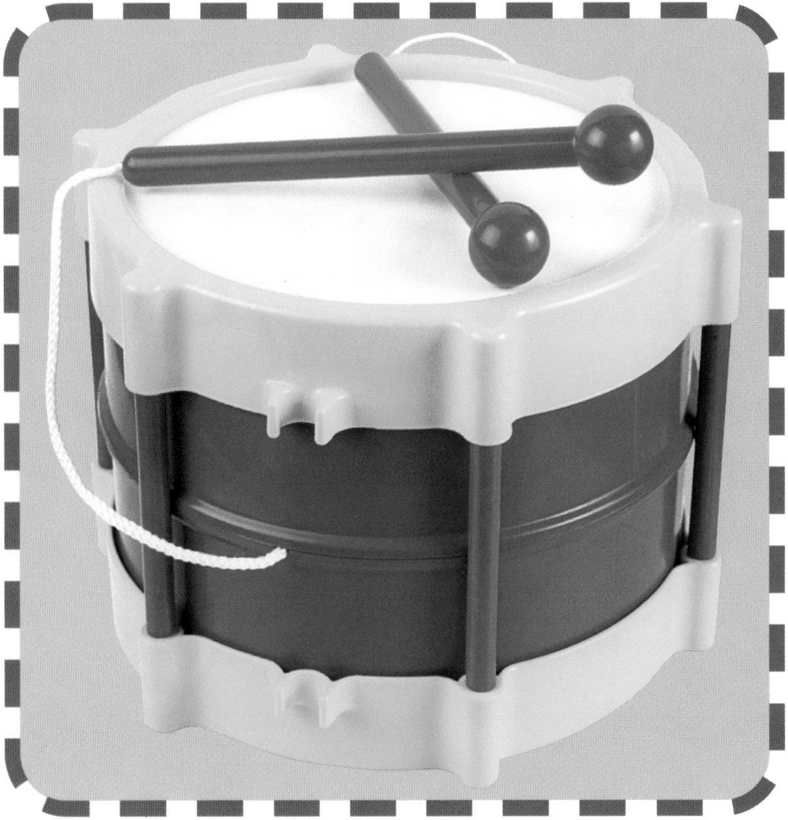

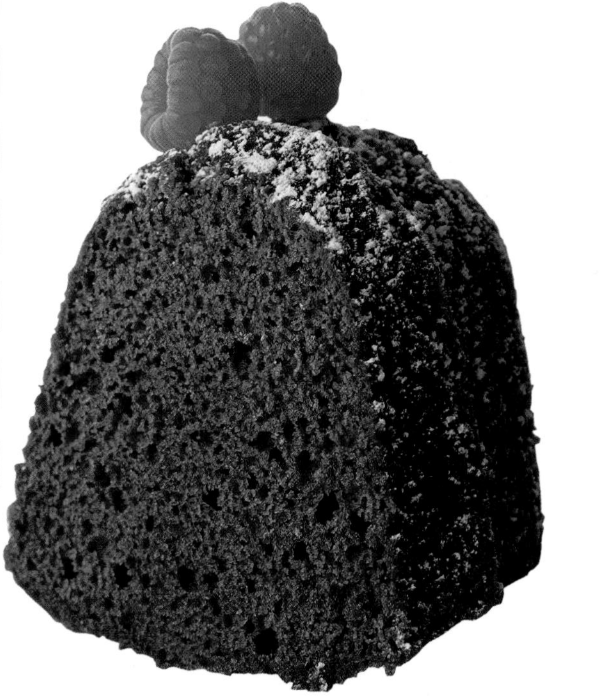

Which one does not belong?

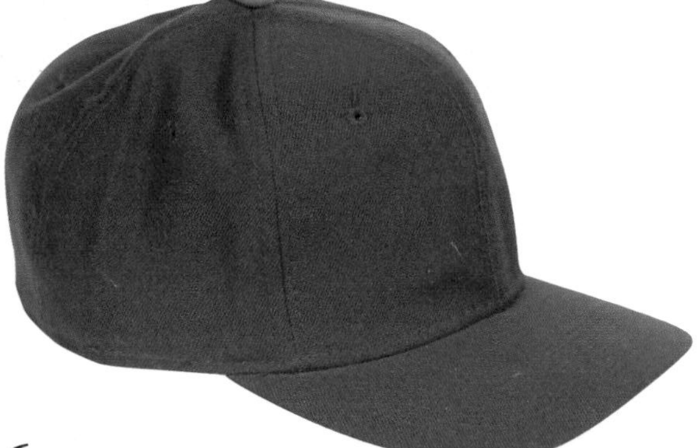

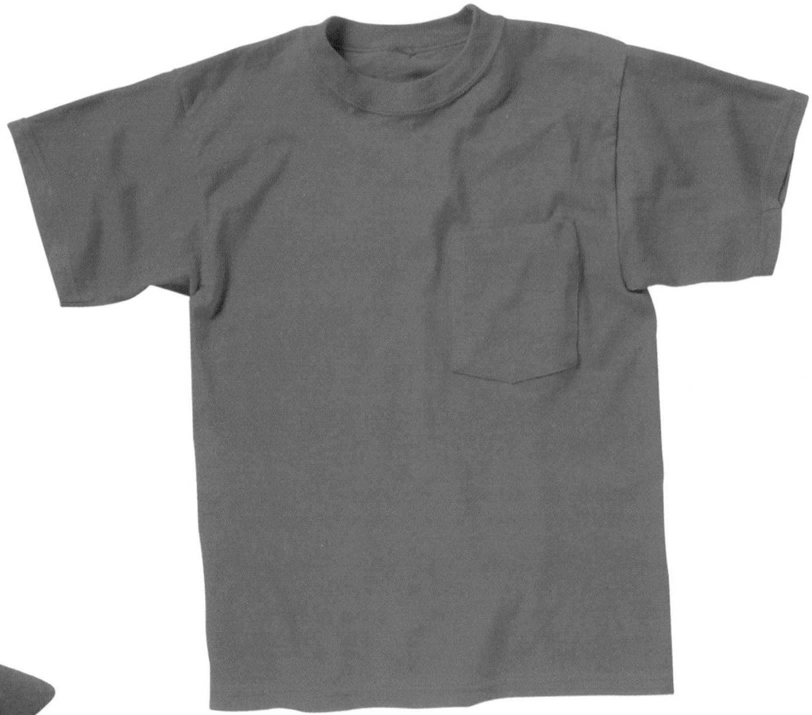

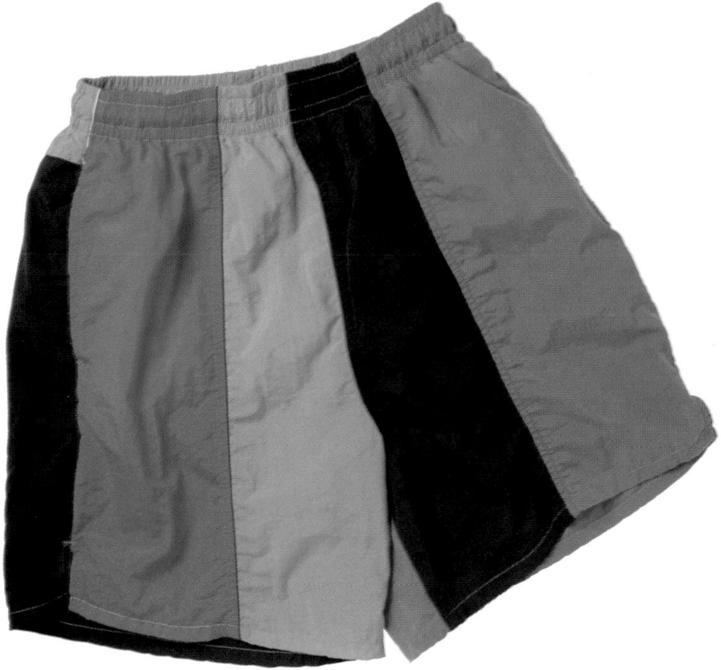

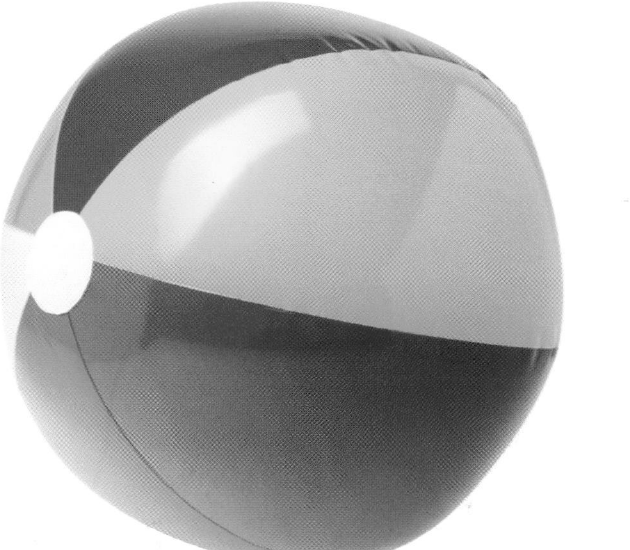

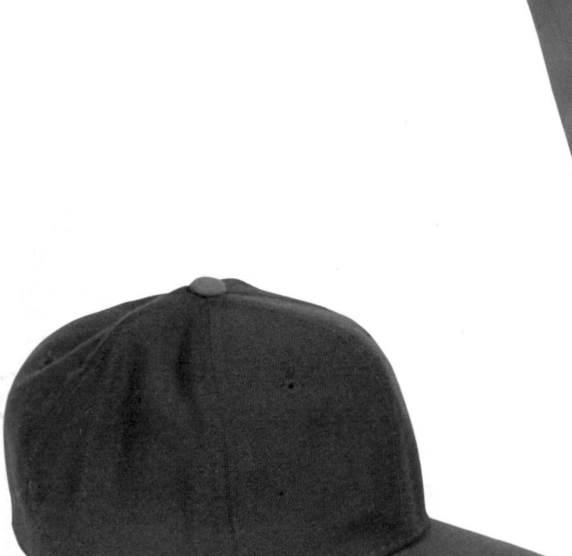

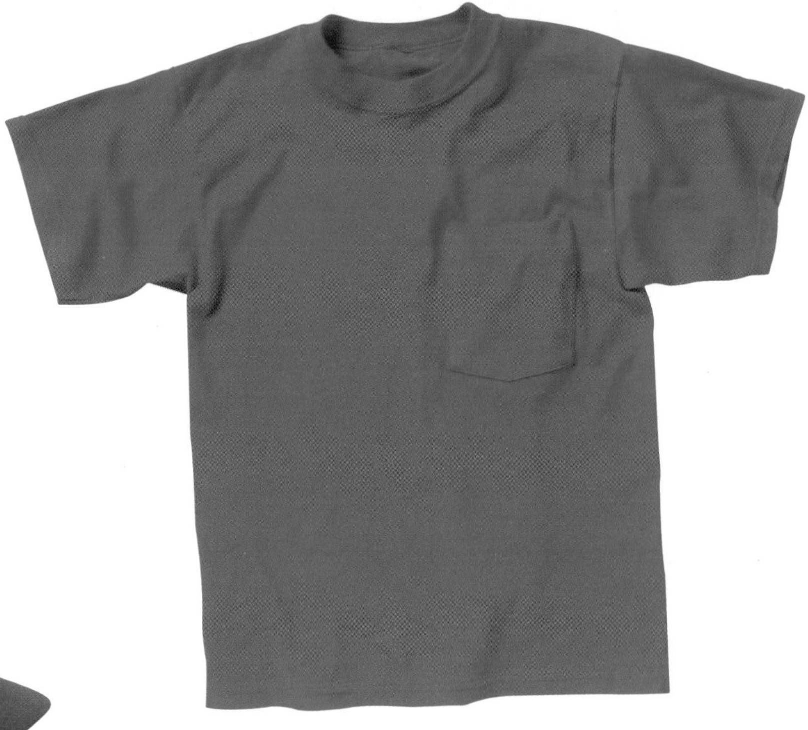

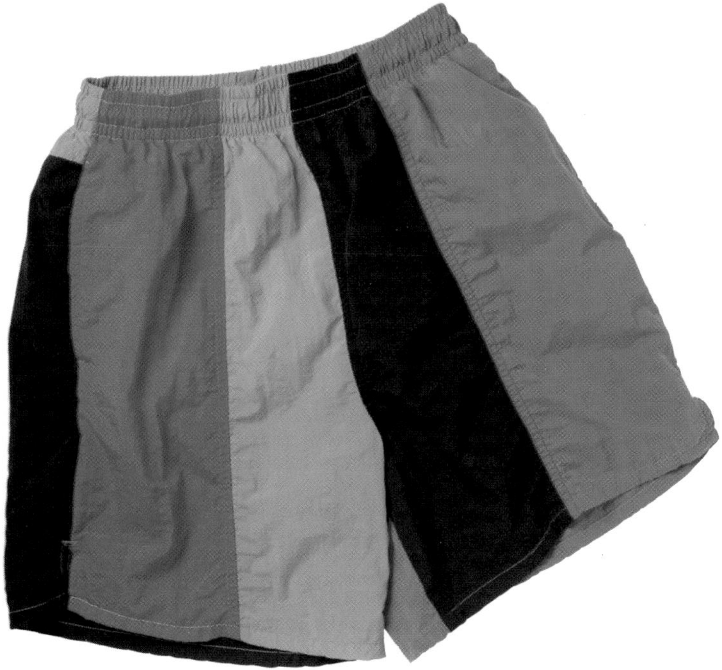

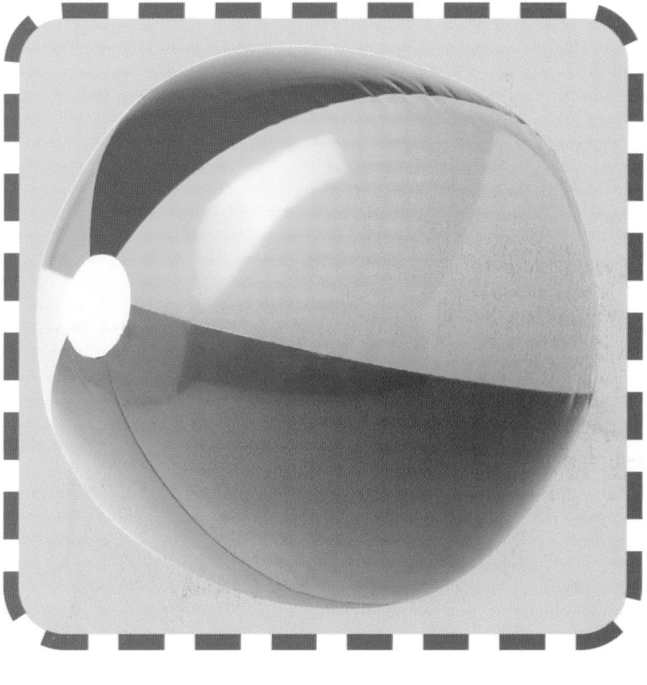

Which one does not belong?

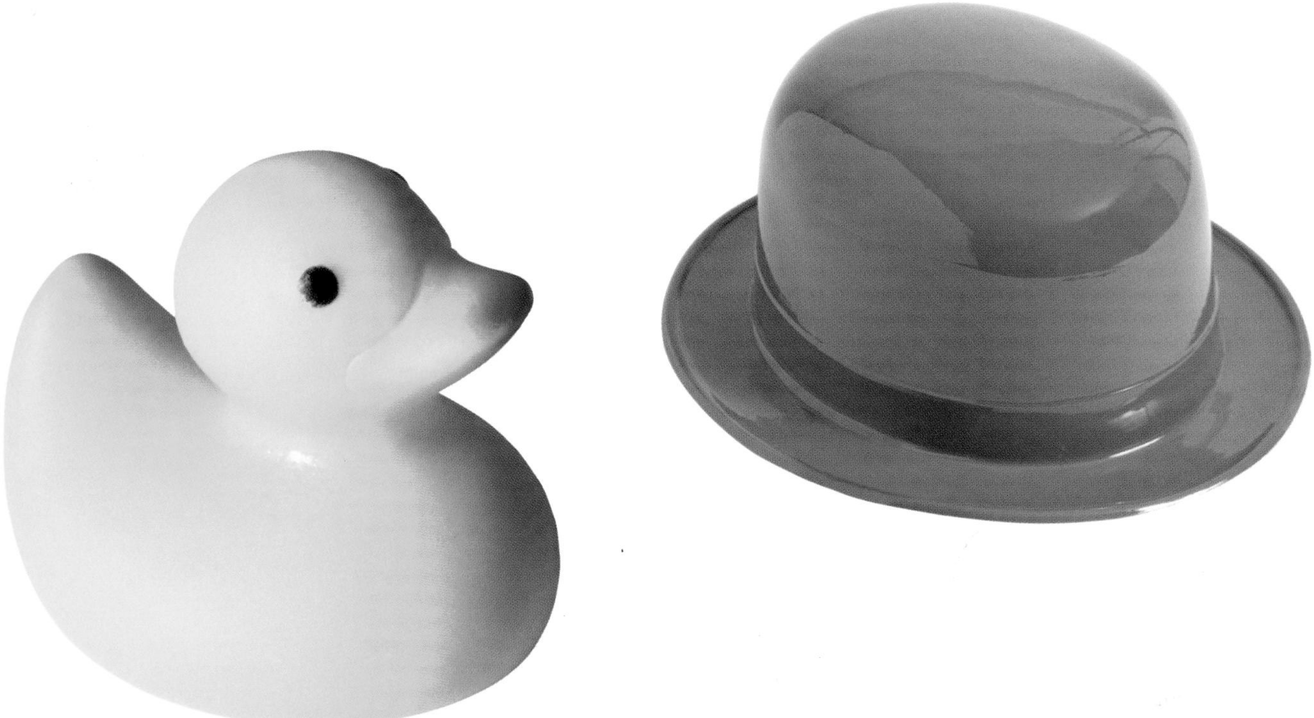

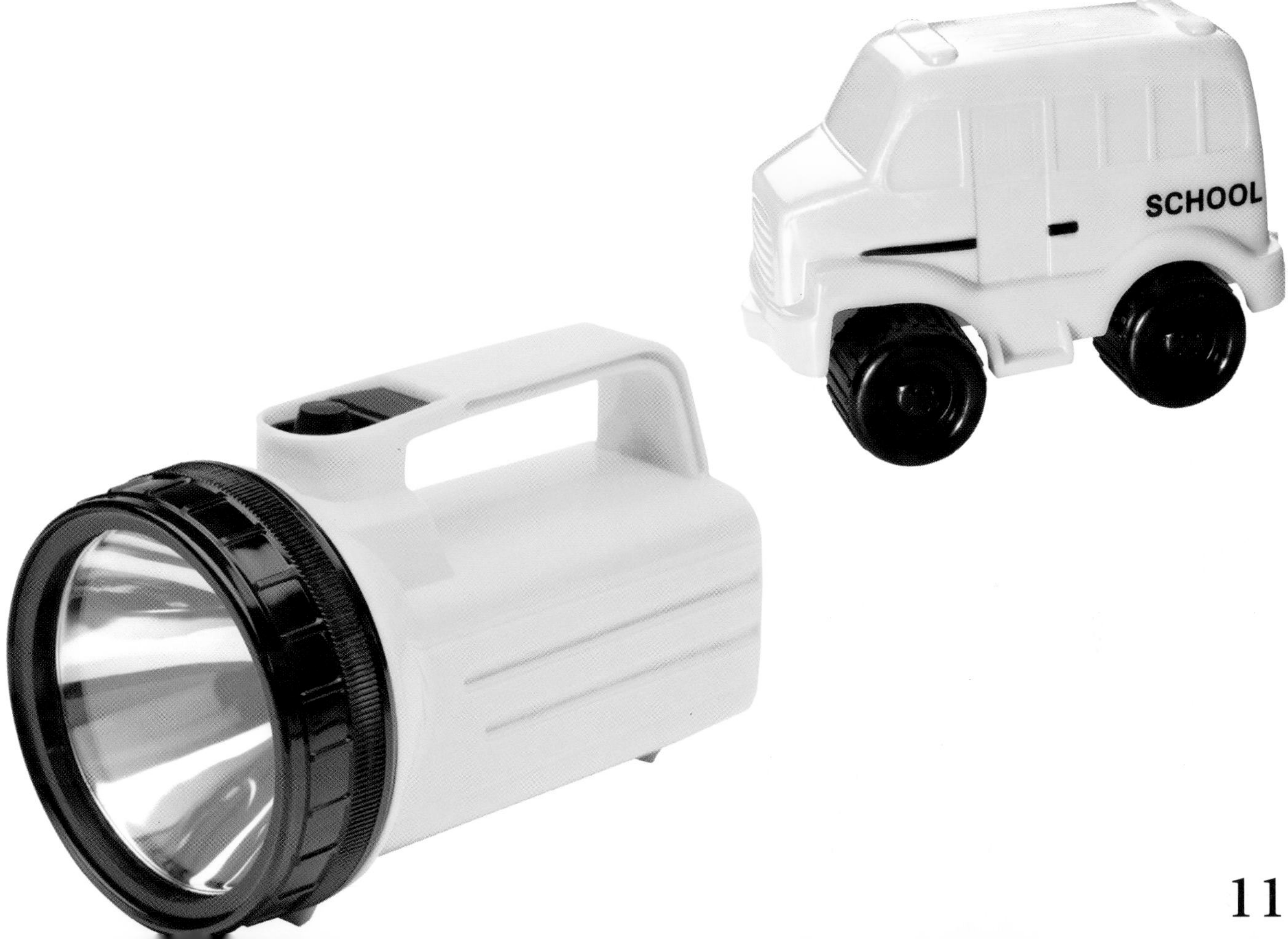
SCHOOL

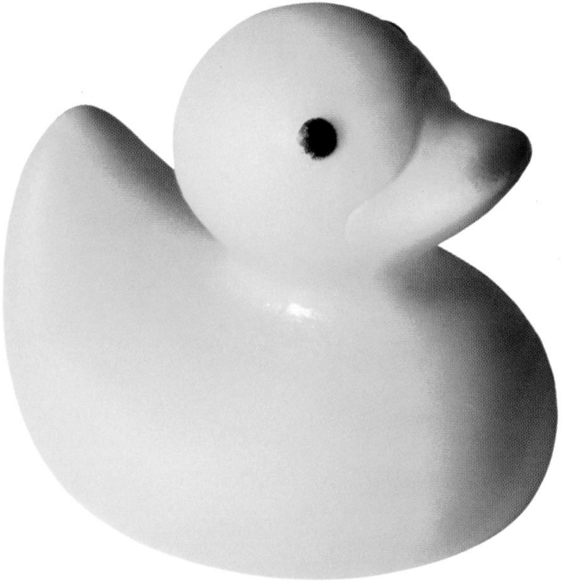

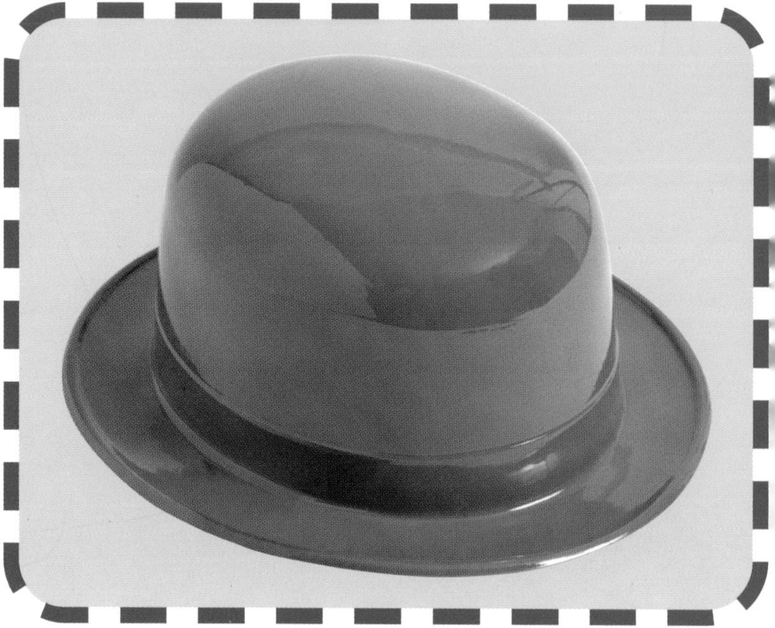

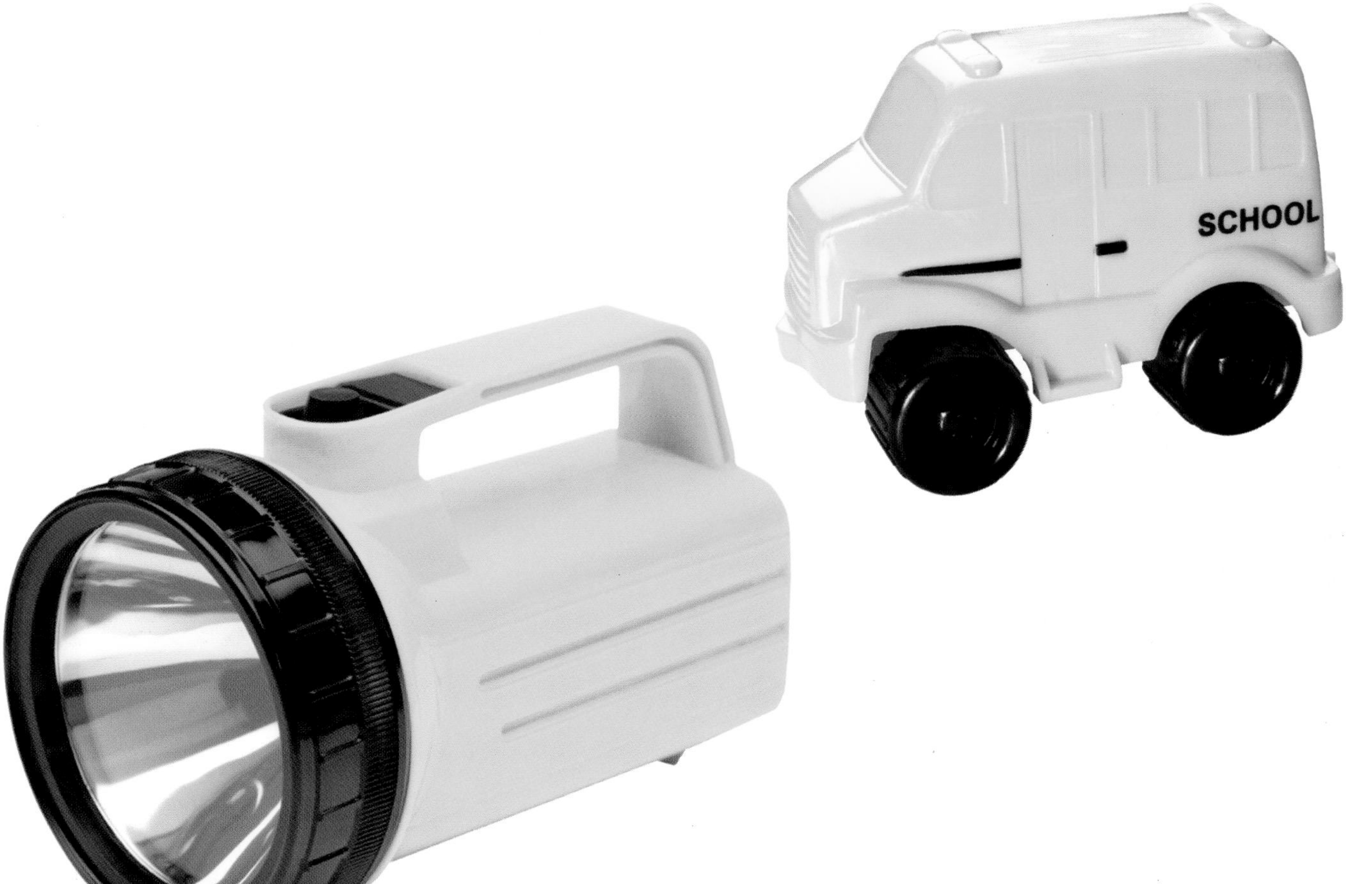
SCHOOL

Which one does not belong?

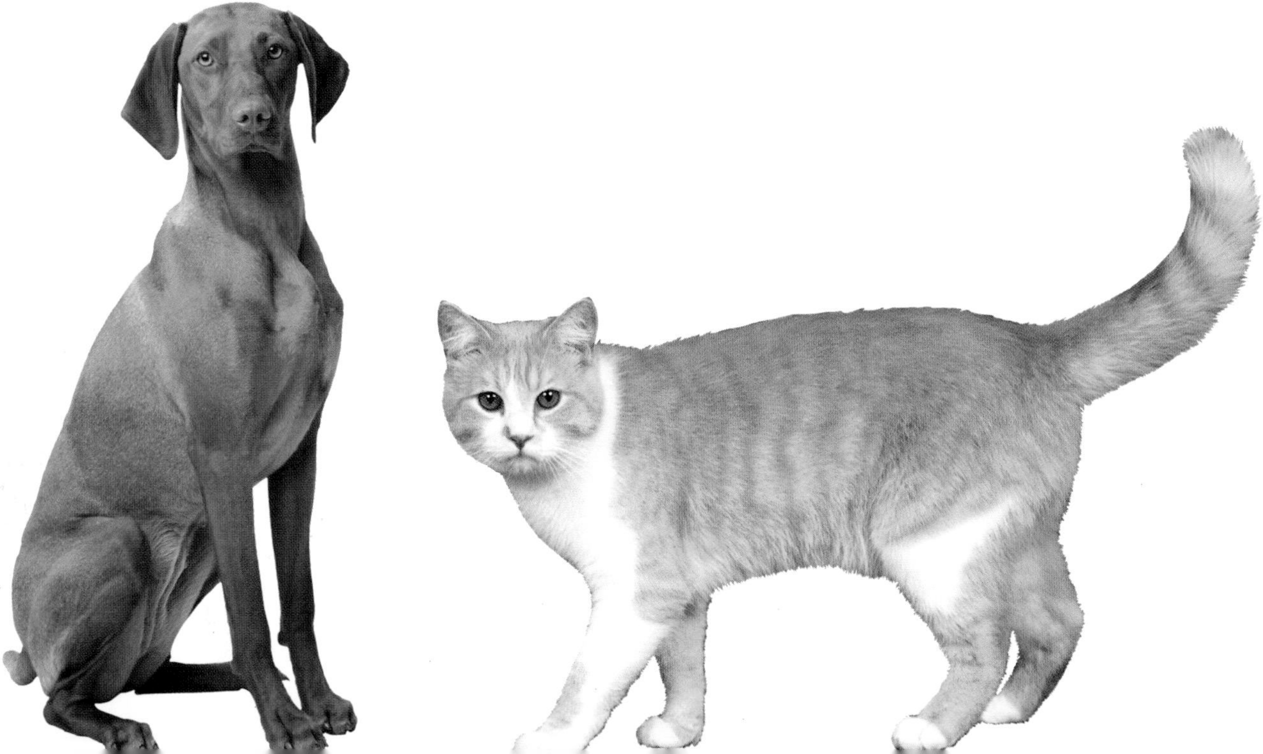

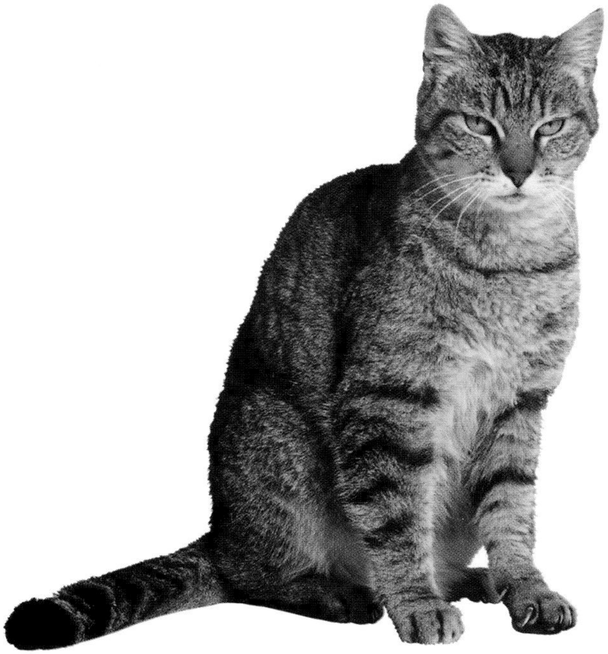

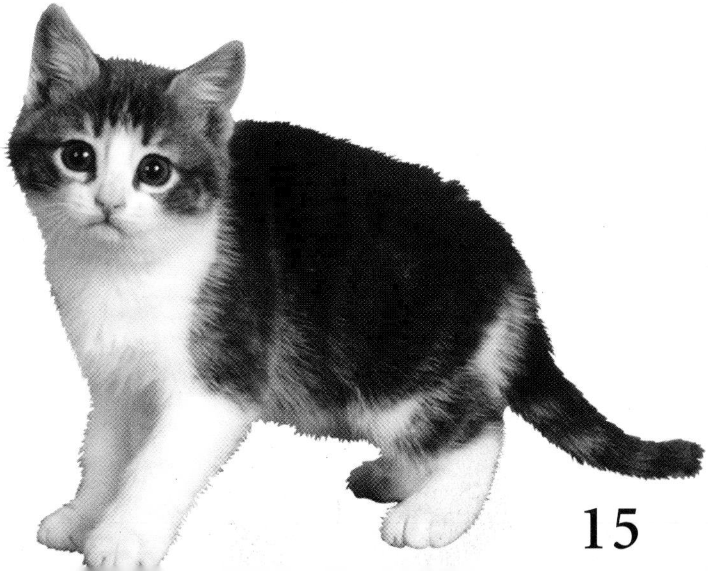

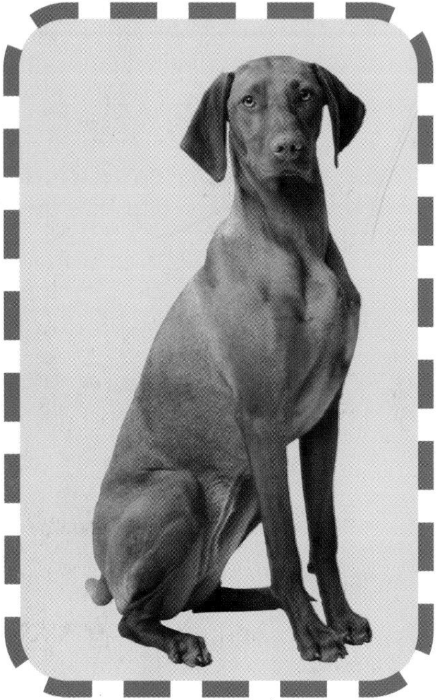

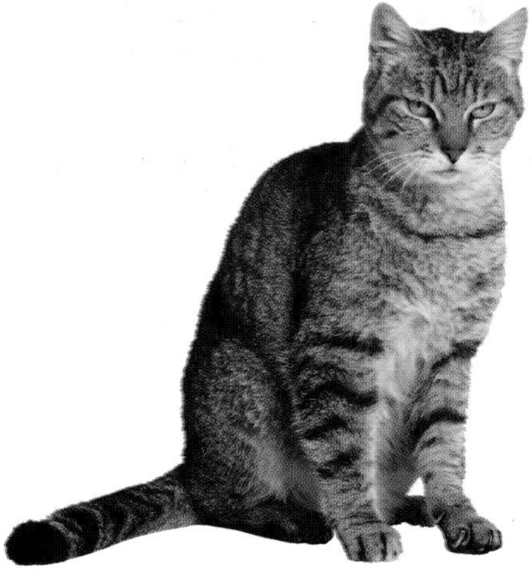

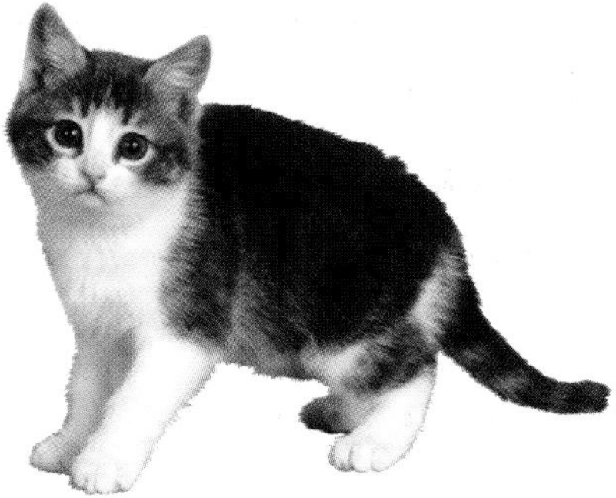

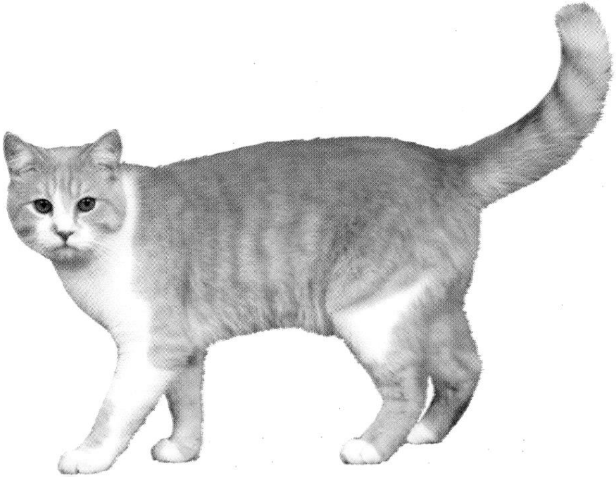